FIERCE
Kindness

Casey;
You are loved.
Love,
Mel

FIERCE
Kindness

BE A POSITIVE FORCE FOR CHANGE

• • • • • • • • • • •

BY MELANIE SALVATORE-AUGUST

Introduction

Fierce Kindness is a way of life: for yourself, for others, for the world. All of life is a choice. We have the power to choose how we think, choose how we create our lives, and choose how we contribute to the world. You may find yourself in circumstances you don't want to be in, but you do not have to be a victim to those circumstances. In any given moment, you can choose how and what you are thinking and begin to create a new version of your life, where you are empowered to be a positive force for change.

This book is about how to be an awesome person to yourself and others. It is clear, direct, and will help you feel good so you can do good out in the world.

Here you will find the tools you need to **redirect your focus from any negativity you are holding to positivity and love, which will in turn transform your life and the way you live it.** I have done it. I do it every day. I choose my life and reroute conditioned, genetic, gender, universal fear-based thinking to love thinking. When I catch myself in old patterns, I pause to use these tools and redirect myself back to positive focus.

Fierce Kindness directs life from feeling unfulfilled to gratitude and abundance. The act of being of service is the key to feeling abundance, and as you begin to shift from being a victim of your circumstances to taking charge of your experience, you will begin to see yourself with greater clarity. **As you realize your power, you will also realize your responsibility to play a larger role for goodness in the world. In fact, the act of being of service will turbo boost the impact of the tools in this book.**
Reciprocal principles:

HELP YOURSELF AND HEAL YOURSELF, HELP OTHERS AND HEAL THE WORLD.

FIERCE:
AUTHENTIC, WILD, STRONG, PASSIONATE, POWERFUL, BRAVE, RED

KINDNESS:
LOVING, COMPASSIONATE, TENDER, GOOD, ALTRUISTIC, TRANSLUCENT

FIERCE KINDNESS

ONE
An action of *powerful goodness*
that shifts the inner conversation
from negative to positive;
problem to possibility; *fear to love.*

TWO
A choice to be *kind—*
especially when it's difficult.

THREE
A movement of nonviolence
and *global consciousness shifting.*

DON'T BELIEVE everything YOU THINK

Don't believe everything you think was the bumper sticker I read out loud when I was twelve years old, zooming down the Pennsylvania Turnpike in my parents' Cadillac Seville. What? I thought that didn't make any sense. What I was thinking was me, wasn't it? Or was it?

In fact, you are not your thoughts. You are *listening* to your thoughts. Now, think about this: if you can listen to them, you can choose to agree or disagree with them. If you can disagree, then you can refute. If you can refute, well then you can change your mind completely and choose where to focus your thoughts.

Note the word *choose*. It's active. It's in your control. *Choose* what helps you get what you want. *Choose* love over fear. Love is all about possibility, positivity, life-giving potential rooted in abundance. Fear is the opposite. It is focused on problems, negativity, dead ends and rooted in scarcity. If you choose to focus your thoughts on abundance and love, it will change you and also allow you to spread that abundant love out in the world.

This book, with its systematic tools, will help you shift your inner conversation from negative to positive, to change your life from a state of reaction and living in fear (in its many forms) to a life that is filled with love (both outward and inward), creating and cultivating a positive inner dialogue and true abundance. The inner work coupled with the outward service will change the entire machination of your life and affect all who come in contact with you.

How to Use This Book

There are several ways to use this book: you can read it from **cover to cover**, or pick it up randomly when you feel discouraged, sad, angry, bored, or hungry and **allow the book to open at random**... and in that moment start there. Write inside this book—all of your heart's questions—with pencil, colored pen, or marker. Please keep this book with you so that instead of reaching for your smart phone or device, **you put pen to paper and help the change begin.**

CHAPTER ONE

THINK

- and -

TAKE
CHARGE

Think:
TO CALL TO ONE'S CONSCIOUS MIND.

TAKE CHARGE:
TO DIRECT, TAKE RESPONSIBILITY FOR, TO HAVE ACCOUNTABILITY.

Now is the time to learn–in the deepest sense– to turn a problem into a possibility. Where you think fear, learn to choose love. Where you think limitation, learn to focus on unbound potential. Note I wrote "think" fear and not "feel" fear, as our thoughts come first and then our emotions. If we can change what and how we think then we can change how we feel. If we can change how we feel then we can change what we do. Change what you do, change your whole life.

You remember that bumper sticker, **Don't believe every-thing you think**? This surprising, radical thought shift is for everyone. You can choose to make the most of your time here on this planet. You can create the life that you want and enjoy all that you have. And you have more than you think. If you are reading these words, you have at least three things to be thankful for: life, the ability to read, and the ability to focus. You most likely have had clean water to drink today, a bed to sleep in, and a roof over your head. Noting the positives and then feeling contentment and gratitude is how we change our minds, our emotions, and our entire lives.

LEARNING THE SKILLED ACTION OF

how to be content

🍂 AND 🍂

how to count my blessings

HAS TURNED MY LIFE AROUND.

IT CAN TURN YOURS AROUND TOO.

THINKING GRATITUDE

to recognize the gift,
to appreciate,
to be awake to the blessing,
to bring to consciousness the goodness
and be thankful.

THINKING ACTION

a skilled movement,
a refined engagement,
a conscious step,
an aware offering.

I grew up with countless blessings but I could not see them. Everywhere I turned was a daily dose of things to fear: there seemed to be scarcity at every corner. There was never enough money, time, resources, attention, success, or love. Competition was the name of the game. *"If you snooze you lose,"* was the saying of the day. It was so not me. I was not aggressive. I was usually last in the line. I would not take that hard hit in dodgeball. I just did not have the killer instincts needed for the dog-eat-dog world and couldn't figure out how to navigate that world without that mindset. That led to deep-rooted anxiety, which fluctuated with depression. I was the girl who had everything but felt I had nothing, and therefore lived in despair.

UNTIL ONE DAY, WHEN A
SMALL CHANGE
STARTED A
PERSONAL
REVOLUTION.

I noticed that *what I concentrated on* developed. Here's what happened (please note it was a mundane, every-day-type happening): I was on a stair-stepper in the San Fernando Valley at an all-women's gym in the late '90s. I had reluctantly begun the monotonous step-step-step and I said to myself, I just can't do this. And you know what? I couldn't. I got off within a minute. I stepped off, took a drink of water and then the thought occurred to me: I wonder what would happen if I say, "I can do it!" instead of I can't? I chuckled because that seemed ridiculous. But then

I thought of the event I had coming up and how I wanted to fit into a certain pair of pants... you know those pants that just barely fit on a good day? So up I went again, step-step-step and I kept saying, "I can do it! I can do it." And I could. I could for the entire twenty-five minutes plus more! It was a small (but incredible) shift and it turned out to be life-transforming.

→ YOU ARE
ACCOUNTABLE
for your
thoughts, feelings,
and life.

Here's the thing: you can do it too. You just have to choose it. You have to want it. Decide to change your mind. It sounds trite and over-simplistic, but amazingly enough, it's true. What do you want? What do you truly desire in your heart? It is up to you. No one can change your mindset for you. Negative thoughts are no one else's fault. Often we want to blame it on our parents or their parents or someone who treated us badly. But it is not *their* fault. You are accountable for your thoughts, feelings, and life. And change will take courage. It will take skilled, step-by-step, consistent action. But first you have to make the decision that you are going to *take charge* of your life and, well, gosh darn it, you are going to shift that sucker from *fear* to *love*; problem to possibility; and scarcity to abundance.

Your thoughts are food. They either nourish you to thrive or poison you to slowly die. You feed whatever you focus on **(attention equals life force)** and reciprocally the areas that you do not feed will weaken and fall away. With this awareness, feed and focus on what you want, what uplifts you, and allow what you do not want to fall away and weaken.

To clarify, it is not a *denial* of the circumstances of your life that are not working. It is a full *acknowledgement* of the circumstances and then a digging down to the thought patterns you're having about those circumstances that are causing you to suffer. In fact denial of the thought, emotion, or experience will perpetuate itself and take you deeper into a negative experience.

As an exercise, take a few minutes and **observe** your thoughts as if from a distance. Next, begin to **direct your attention** to something you love or that you are grateful for. Notice how your breath and body **feel**. Switch your attention to something that frightens you or is a concern; again notice your breath and body. You controlled the direction of your mind and the feelings that accompanied that focus. Now purposefully process how you think about specific circumstances in your life and the feelings that go with those circumstances. Next, observe what actions you are taking *because* of your feelings. And now you ***know* the feelings that are driving your actions!** In other words, you now understand why you are living/doing/saying what you are. That's step one.

ONLY YOU

CAN CHANGE YOUR THINKING

AND THEREBY

CHANGE YOUR LIFE.

NO ONE ELSE CAN.

Once you begin to live out that concept of being account-able for your experience, you are on your way to your most abundant life. You are a self-cleaning oven: process what is good and burn off what does not serve the greater good of you and the world.

Here's one example that may be of help. Let's say you have a job you like, but you're too busy, with too much on your plate. You may view it as overwhelming, or you may view it as an exciting professional challenge. The difference in your viewpoint will tremendously affect your perception of how your job is going. It's the same job; it's the same you. The difference is in your thoughts about it. One is positive, one is negative.

Build on that clarity: you have the power to pause and notice if you are focusing on the negative and feeling like a victim, or viewing your circumstances through a positive lens and believing you are in charge and creating your experience. If it's the former, purposefully reframe. Rework and create a new, positive, empowered thought pattern. The power to pause the momentum and **move your thoughts from problem to possibility** will allow you to **awaken to the best life you can live.**

In the next chapters, we will explore how to **pause, listen,** and **reframe.** The great news is that it gets easier and easier the more you do it, so don't give up: **keep going.**

CHAPTER TWO:

DISCERN

- and -

BE HEARD

DISCERN:

TO RECOGNIZE, DISTINGUISH, OR PERCEIVE.

Be heard:

TO BE ACKNOWLEDGED, WITNESSED, HEEDED, UNDERSTOOD.

Your past experiences and perceptions have shaped who you are today. There is also an aspect of you—a *core self*, your essence—that has remained constant, never changing along the way. The *core self* is you: you as spirit, soul, or pure life awareness. You are the constant that dreams, perceives the thoughts, feels the emotions, and observes the body.

Although the deepest sense of your *core self* is set, you can continue learning how to direct your thoughts and actions. This is where, at times, our society and our world influence our thoughts and choices for better or worse. This is the conflict that we all are faced with, when at a certain point in our lives we realize that we are making choices based on outside influence or pressure instead of our essential wisdom. **This realization of being out of alignment is the first and most powerful step.** Next, you need to pause and connect to what you really want in your life. Is there misalignment with this desire and focus? If there is, you will need to learn to shift your direction. That learning to direct yourself is where true power and content-ment come from. As we get better at creating positive focus based in our *core selves*, then we will feel more content and our actions will have more authentically rooted power.

You are always listening to your thoughts, even when another part of you is busy doing something else. I call this "underlying chatter" and it's important to realize it is happening and **notice what messages you are telling yourself.** Are the messages affirming, or contributing to a negative self-image? By bringing consciousness to these conditioned messages, we *take charge* of the messages we give ourselves.

It is simple yet not easy, and like physical exercise, the more you do it, the stronger you will become.

At one point you may have believed everything your mind said to you; now you know to be suspicious.

QUESTION
YOUR
THOUGHTS.

Challenge your thoughts, and if they are rooted in negativity then consciously redirect them to something nutritious, kind, and positive. Here's an example: "I hate washing the dishes" verses "I am thankful that I have food to eat and therefore dishes to clean." It's the same dishes and same you but a shifted perspective; one negative, with a dead-end energy, and one positive, with possibility for growth. Note the use of gratitude, as the act of appreciation is a powerful redirector.

There are two channels or frequencies: one positive that energizes us, which I call the love channel, and one negative that shuts us down, which I call the fear channel.

This shift of perspective from negative to positive is, at its root, a turning of *fear* to *love*.

THE SHIFT IS WHERE TRUE TRANSFORMATION HAPPENS.

FEAR-CHANNEL THOUGHT

One rooted in fear of not having enough,
rooted in pain, negativity,
scarcity, judgment, tightness,
restriction, chaos, murk, disturbance,
destruction, steeped in problems
and unpleasantness.
Holds information for growth.

LOVE-CHANNEL THOUGHT

One rooted in love and having everything
that is needed, rooted in pleasure,
positivity, abundance,
compassion, spaciousness, life giving,
peace, clarity, creativity,
steeped in possibility and goodness.
The channel of *core self* and intuitive
wisdom where highest power happens.

The key to this growth and transformation in ourselves, and in turn of the world, is to listen and process what is in the fear channel and use it as fuel. This fuel strengthens our ability to shift our thoughts from the negative fear channel to the positive love channel, which is the frequency of *core self*. **When your intuition or higher wisdom talks to you, it speaks through the love channel.** Understand that these two channels of thought work separately from each other; generally you cannot be in both at the same time. You may argue that you can feel happy about something *but* also have a nagging worry it will end. I will debate that there is only one thought at a time and the first thought is present in the positive (and it created a happy feeling); and then the negative thought follows. Two different thoughts—not at the same time, *but* consecutive. First get clear that there are TWO channels and then practice pausing to listen, to feel, and to *discern* which channel or frequency your particular thought is on.

Words are powerful and carry a frequency, as in the above paragraph where the word *but* acts as a disruptor of positive, creative flow. *But* makes an immediate conflict and is rooted in a lack of power and disconnection. "I want this, *but* I don't have the power to have it." So notice when you mentally use the word *but*, and then redirect yourself if a negative thought has followed the positive.

Like attracts like, and when you shift yourself to the love channel—which holds possibility and abundance—then possibility and abundance will come to you. **We attract what we are, not necessarily what we want, so actively shifting your thoughts will raise your vibration and the experiences you bring into your life.**

If your thought is on the fear channel (which is, by nature, about not having enough), acknowledge it then take charge and redirect your mind to a positive thought (which is by nature about having what you need). "My happiness fortifies me *and* I will live in the moment." If a circumstance comes in which there is pain, trust that you will be strong and capable enough to handle the pain in a positive, affirming way. Example: "Although my ankle is broken, I am in the care of a good doctor and have friends around to help me." (Again, note gratitude here.) Note the perception of the circumstances. Take charge of your thinking to stay in the positive, emotionally nutritious thought zone.

Like healthy food,
NUTRITIONAL THOUGHTS
will fortify you.

PACK UP YOUR TOOL KIT

**There are simple, powerful tools
to move out of the fear channel and shift into love.**

STEP 1

Pause, feel, and observe your thought

• • • • • • • • • • •

STEP 2

Identify the channel of your thought

• • • • • • • • • • •

STEP 3

Take charge of your thoughts
(by connecting to your *core self*)

• • • • • • • • • • •

STEP 4

Shift your thoughts from *fear* to *love*

STEP 1: Pause, feel, and observe your thoughts

You do this by consciously pausing throughout your day to listen to yourself. Once you can hear and identify the messages you are feeding yourself, notice whether they are nutritious, positive thoughts, or poisonous, negative thoughts. If they're the latter, purposefully switch them (clear tools for this ahead.) Remember this is a moment-to-moment practice, not a magic pill to wash over an entire day, week, or life. A life of *fierce kindness* is built from a foundation of moments, and we can become mindful of our moments along with our thoughts and breaths in order to live our ideal lives.

STEP 2: Identify the channel of the thought

How do you know what thoughts to heed and which to discard and redirect? You can identify the channel of thought by feeling, listening, as well as asking yourself the right questions. If the message is one of possibility—that there is enough to go around and that you are a part of a loving universe—you are in the love channel and on the right frequency. If the thought is based in scarcity—that there is not enough to go around, or that you are a victim of the circumstance—then you know you are heading in the wrong direction as you are in the fear channel.

Listen to what you say to yourself as well as what you say to other people, which is often the easiest place to catch a negative channel. Both of these conversations indicate what channel you are in, and if the message is a conditioned, negative one you'll know by some key words and actions that are big flags for negativity:

CATCH THE NEGATIVE PHRASES AND CONVERSATIONS

Have to
Should
But
Always / never / everything
Complaining
Blaming others for your experience: "You made me feel..."
Petty judgments and nitpicking
Comparisons (as someone is always going to come up short)
Gossip

Words have power and sometimes they are used casually or carelessly. By catching your negative phrases you will plug up leaks of negative spill and get insight into your current channel. You don't "have to," you *choose* to, even when it's difficult. You are choosing to do whatever is to be done, and when you take full accountability for the choice you will open up possibility. You *should, but* you don't want to? Why are you doing things you do not want to do? **You deserve a better life than one that is filled with unconscious choices you don't actually want.** Choose to go to work and be thankful that you are able to put food in your children's mouths. Catch the "have to," the "should," the "but," and anything else that is in this line of victimhood.

Don't let the negative self-talk or inner bully push you around. Oftentimes the recording of inner doubt or criticism has been playing since childhood. The seed of this weed called doubt may have been planted by an early challenge or trauma. It can be helpful to identify where the root of this self-talk comes from (without getting stuck on it) and then move into catching it and shifting it to something helpful. That inner voice may say that you aren't good, smart, or cool enough, and weave fear into your *core self*'s vision and purpose. Don't let it rule you, catch it and with the love of a grown child remind yourself that you are not only enough, **you are more than enough,** and then move on. My inner bully will tell me that I am weird, too sensitive, and don't fit in. From wisdom and experience I know now that my *weirdness* and *sensitivity* are my gifts to the world as they helps me see things at a different angle from the norm and these exact skills help me be a thought leader of goodness in my community. This is a re-writing of a personal story, shifting from victim to creator, follower to leader. Often **our greatest gifts to the world are the lessons we have learned from overcoming our challenges and shifting our inner bully.** My inner bully has become my cheerleader and my pain has shifted to my power of purpose.

WE HAVE
TWO EYES, TWO EARS
– AND –
only ONE *mouth*
FOR A REASON:
COMPASSIONATELY OBSERVE MORE,
SPEAK LESS.

Consider reducing the amount of careless chatter or small talk you may do within a day. By reducing the amount, you will create more space to listen to your *core self* and be more accurate and powerful in what you do say to create abundance.

We have two eyes, two ears and one mouth for a reason: compassionately observe more, speak less. A helpful filter for the words you do choose is:

.... IS IT *true*?

.... IS IT *kind*?

.... IS IT *helpful*?

.... IS IT *necessary*?

The use of silence with observation and the above filter will help you choose your words with greater potency and greatly increase your effectiveness in all areas of life.

SILENCE

IS ALMOST ALWAYS APPROPRIATE

(UNTIL IT IS NOT, AND IT IS TIME TO CONSCIOUSLY LEAD).

Pause, feel, and observe your thoughts to **discern**.
Observe how it feels physically as well as emotionally.
Your *core self* will call you to connection, compassion, possibility, and an expansive state of unconditional love.

What does that feel like? Go back to the exercise from chapter one of stopping, breathing, closing your eyes to think of something you love or that you are grateful for. Feel that expansive sense in your breathing, your chest cavity, how your belly relaxes and your chin lifts upward.

Now in opposition, think about something that really scares you: note the tightness in your breath, your chest, and belly; you may tuck your chin slightly or contract in your shoulders, neck, and jaw.

The body knows what channel the mind is on. Take time throughout the day to pause and listen to your body, especially when you are at any crossroads and need to make a decision. Taking time to discern the root of the internal message will begin to dramatically shift how you feel and your experience of the world for the better. The more you do it, the better and more sensitive you will become to the cues.

STEP 3: Take charge of your thoughts
(by connecting to your core self)

Question your feelings and thoughts by asking yourself
key questions to prompt *core self* wisdom to come through.
Your *core self* will lead you in the direction of what is
life-giving, or simply put, to love.

Ask yourself:

What is it that I genuinely want?

What do I need right now?

What is most important to the big picture in
this moment?

What are my choices here? Which is based in
fear and which is based in love?

What would (Buddha, Jesus, Mother Theresa,
Gandhi, someone I deeply admire) do?

Sometimes fill-in-the-blank can be very helpful:

If I could (do, say, have) whatever I wanted right now, it would be_____.

All I really want to feel is_____.

All I really want is_____.

If I could create whatever I wanted, it would be
_____.

I want to let go of_____.

The most important thing for me and all involved is _____.

Ask your *core self* and guiding power for clarity and support:

Please talk to me Heart (Love, Universe, God). I am listening.

Show me the way.

Guide my heart and I will follow.

Guide me to the highest and best outcome for all involved.

The **power is in the pause,** because without pausing or stopping to check in with your thoughts/feelings then the spinning wheel of reaction will keep spinning. You know, "He said that to me, so I said that back, and then he yelled and we bickered which made me late so I had to hurry, and then because I hurried, I forgot my purse. I forgot my purse and had to turn around halfway to work. I was late for work and hysterical because my boss said one more tardy and I'm out of there. I stuck my head out of the window and yelled at the slow car in front of me..."

It keeps going and going and going. Until you stop.

STOP
and
REFOCUS
TO IDENTIFY
THE CHANNEL OF THOUGHT

Information is in the body. Pause all movement, and focus on your breathing to feel how you feel. Slow your breath down and inhale through your nose and out of your mouth and then take inventory of your state of being. How do you feel both physically and emotionally? Are you in a negative spin? **What is it that your deep core self really wants? Is it love? Ease? Spaciousness? Listen to that.** The act of pausing, breathing, and feeling so you can listen to your *core self* will begin the process of resetting yourself into positivity. Sometimes the feeling or emotion can be quite strong, so a bit of surfing is needed. **Emotions are temporary,** and riding the wave of an emotion—allowing it to crest and then diminish—is helpful to get to that more anchored place of creator. Emotions by nature are in a state of movement, which is important to remember because **no matter how bad you feel in the moment, *it will pass.*** Allow for this natural progression or wave, and explore some of the following tools to help move through to the next step of processing.

STEP 4: Shift your thoughts from *fear* to *love*

You *take charge* of your experience by listening to your *core self* wisdom and aligning your actions with that. When your *core self* is being heard and heeded you will attract the goodness that lives in the love channel. Now that you are clear that a shift is needed, here are some ways to shift, shake off, and get in the zone of *fierce kindness*.

HERE ARE SOME OTHER ACTIONS TO SHIFT INTO A POSITIVE FRAME OF MIND:

1. **UTILIZE AN AFFIRMATION OR MANTRA** to put yourself in the desired state of mind—for example, repeat out loud or silently, *"I am enough,"* *"I have everything I need,"* or *"I trust the timing."*

2. **CHANGE YOUR TONE** Purposefully change the way you are speaking to yourself and others by speaking with clear intention and catching the negative before-mentioned catch phrases: *"I have to do the dishes"* to *"I am choosing to do the dishes now."*

SWITCH LOCATIONS Move your physical body out of a negative place or situation. If you are inside, go outside. If you're in the company of a negative person or a negative influence, remove yourself from that and get to a new location. This simple but powerful tool of *changing it up* works wonders.

3

GO FROM DRY TO WET A bath or shower can completely shift a perspective (helps soothe children, too!).

4

GET STILL, rooted, and silent.

5

GO FROM STILL TO MOVING Like stopping your action to be still, switching yourself to a motion such as walking, running, practicing yoga, or other physical activity can help.

6

CHANGE THE VIBE Put on uplifting music, yawn, sigh loudly, sing, *OM* and dance, run in circles, jump up and down. Change to the opposite and shift the negative to the positive.

7

take a shower or bath

run

say oh well and let it go

jump

stop and drink a glass of water

dance

change your location

cry

M
S
HA

laugh it off

sing, chant OM, sigh loudly

stretch

look up to the sky, hug a tree, walk barefoot in the grass

pause to get quiet and still

journal

put on music

gratitude

KE
FT
PEN

*A note on gratitude:

USE IT GENEROUSLY,
AS IT IS THE
GREAT NEGATIVITY CUTTER.

TRAIN TO SHIFT
ANY MOMENT

to one of

APPRECIATION

AND WATCH IT

BLOOM

INTO MORE ABUNDANCE.

It may seem like an overly simple solution to choose positivity over negativity and thereby fix your life, but amazingly enough, that's how it all begins. Help yourself, help the world: it only takes one voice and it starts with you.

In the words of Martin Luther King Jr.,

"DARKNESS
CANNOT DRIVE OUT DARKNESS,
only light can do that.
HATE CANNOT DRIVE OUT HATE;
only love can do that."

CHAPTER THREE

COURAGE

- to -

FOCUS

Courage:

BRAVERY FUELED BY AN ALIGNMENT WITH THE HEART

FOCUS:

TO CONCENTRATE ON, TO BRING ATTENTION TO, THE CENTER OF INTEREST; FOCAL POINT

In chapters one and two, the transformation began: you learned to identify negative self-talk and switch it to positive. You learned the steps you can take to accomplish that end.

Now it's time to focus on what you can do with your newfound power. It begins with taking a good, hard look at how you perceive yourself. Where do you find your intrinsic value? How you value yourself is the anchor to the lasting process of *fierce kindness.*

Circumstances in your life will constantly change. You may be married now, but weren't in the past, and may not be in the future. You may have a job you love or hate, or may not be working at all. Know that your circumstances do not define you. You are not your body, gender, money, relationships, or education. You are not your talents or even your mental capabilities. You are your *core self*, and that self is good. You are at a perfect starting point and will, if you allow yourself to do so, continue to develop as you learn to live in the love channel.

Once you determine how you identify yourself, note whether your perception may be causing negative thinking, and therefore personal suffering. If that's the case, **re-focus your thoughts based on the new definition of who you are: your *core self* based in love.**

Create
A NEW HABIT

As with any habit, the more you do it, the more it strengthens, so creating positive habits is the key to *fierce kindness*: first for yourself and then for the world. Ideally you will create a positive, pleasurable feedback loop through your thinking that radiates out into your whole body. As a reminder, your thoughts either nourish you to thrive or poison you to slowly die. Your food is whatever you focus on **(attention equals life force)** and reciprocally the areas that you do not feed will weaken and fall away.

Create the habit of pausing and reminding yourself that you are in charge of your thoughts and how you focus them. It only takes one positive thought to change an action; one person to shift the course of events, and that person is you. In this way begin to build a foundational habit of listening to your highest self and aligning your focus with that.

WHAT YOU FOCUS ON

EXPANDS.

WHAT YOU THINK ABOUT,

you create.

YOUR THOUGHTS MANIFEST

YOUR EMOTIONS AND

PHYSICAL WELL-BEING.

YOUR LIFE

WILL MIRROR

WHAT AND HOW YOU THINK.

YOUR LIFE

is a culmination of all your thoughts and experiences

UP TO THIS POINT.

In my early twenties, I was a new inhabitant of New York City and I was experiencing a great amount of fear and anxiety. I was worried about making it in the city. I was afraid I might not have what it took to reach my goals. This fear about my future and lack of power in my present vibrated out of me in great waves. I exuded the fear of an animal in survival mode.

Because I was so attuned to my own suffering, when I looked out to the world around me that is all I saw in return. In fact, the frightening nature of the world led me to stay in my tiny, dark basement apartment. I was afraid to leave it and when I did venture out to the market or to work I was met with negative experiences. I was groped on the crammed subway, shoved out of the way in Times Square, barked at by a passerby. I could not believe that anyone could possibly love that city and actually want to stay there by choice.

I was constantly planning my exit: once I got my career together...once I met the man of my dreams...once I refined my talents, I was out of there.

One day I overheard someone saying that the **city was simply a reflection of whatever was going on inside each person** and that if you were in love with your life, you would be in love with the city; conversely, if you were suffering in your life you would see suffering everywhere around you.

I was incredulous; it was like the *Don't believe everything you think* bumper sticker and I was confounded by it. How could this be? I was not creating the ugliness around me. Or was I?

At that point, **I began to play a game with myself** whenever I walked out of my apartment: **I would consciously invoke a thought of love and gratitude and I would then look for something outside to confirm it.** I was shocked and delighted that whenever I played this game I would end up smiling. Truly smiling from the inside out, and you know what? People smiled back at me. I saw beautiful mothers, innocent children, playful merchants, and kindness around me. I also began to look in the mirror and do the same; I looked for the good. I began to train my inner and outer eyes to focus on what was good instead of what was lacking.

I didn't realize that the game I was playing was the groundwork to understanding the law of attraction. I was raised to be *discerning* because from discernment came power and *safety*. I understood this discernment to be about seeing what was lacking in any given situation and then being able to fix or avoid it. My eyes had been trained to find what was wrong in a situation; to create safety nets and escape routes. I believed that focusing on the perceived threats around me would help me make wise choices.

This learned way of looking to find the threat was not in alignment with my *core self* and true nature. My true nature was to **see beauty, be curious,** and **trust the magnificence of goodness.** Being out of alignment with my *core self* was causing me to suffer. Many of my choices were based on this denial, and because of that I felt lost and powerless. **I had to get fierce with myself and bravely step into alignment to follow my heart.**

I HAD TO
TRAIN MY EYE
to see what was good
IN ANY SITUATION.

The more I chose to see the positive and acted on this trust of abundance instead of scarcity, the stronger I got. The success and pleasure of this feedback loop kept reinforcing the habit, and that changed my life. This repetition increased my bravery, and with small step-by-step actions I realigned my life into the light of my heart and *core self*.

My successful experiences with the law of attraction proved that trying to live in a positive world, while focusing on the negatives around me, was not possible. I had to undo years of conditioned patterns and retrain my eye to see what was good in any situation. At my core I am a creature rooted in love and a child of god. Living in this way allowed my heart to feel safe and have the courage to offer my innate gifts to the world.

This is the thought-emotion-action cycle. It happens over and over. It is the building block of the experience of your life and your interaction with the world. The circumstance of how you live may still happen, but the experience will be different. We can choose where we concentrate our focus. In the famous words of Haruki Murakami, "Pain is inevitable; suffering is optional." So choose not to suffer. The suffering will attract more suffering. The cycle of the mind being in fear and blame will act like a boomerang and attract more of that back into your experience.

CHOOSING TO BE **CURIOUS AND CONTENT**
IN YOUR CURRENT CIRCUMSTANCES
— AND FOCUSING ON —
the possibilities that lie ahead
ARE THE KEYS TO THE LAW OF ATTRACTION
AND THE ROOT OF *FIERCE KINDNESS.*

STEP 1: Be curious about the circumstances at hand instead of being swept away in any kind of negative reaction.

STEP 2: Begin to explore with a sense of detached interest the uncomfortable nature of what you are experiencing. Train yourself to become comfortable with being uncomfortable, curious in your own processing, so you can see the opening to shift whatever you are experiencing into something positive and nourishing.

STEP 3: Choose to be happy. Often we think that once we achieve our goal or ideal circumstance then we will be happy. It is actually the opposite: when you choose to be content, then you will be happy and will attract the highest outcome for yourself and those connected to you. Your thinking will make you more creative, resourceful, powerful and effective in overcoming your circumstances and current obstacles, and will make you more attractive to positive people who naturally seek relationships with other positive people.

STEP 4: Step forward in faith. Your choice to be curious, content and positive is like a beautiful shiny red apple. This apple will be nutritious and delicious for you as long as there is not a worm in it. The worm is doubt. Once the worm is in the apple, it is no longer good for you. As one of my goodness heroes Suzanne Conrad says, "Doubt is the operating system of Fear, and Faith is the operating system of Love." When you catch doubt, which may come in the form of the inner bully to diminish your belief in living in the positive, then go to a shift tool. Redirect it, purge it, remind it of your clear understanding that *like attracts like* and for you to create the life your *core self* dreams of then you must create solely from the love channel and clear all doubt aside.

YOU GET WHAT YOU GIVE,
so give love away.

Now that you are in the groove of positive thinking and focus for yourself—give it away. Take conscious action to give more than you take and give without expectation of return. Think *fierce compassion*. Take your positive thoughts beyond yourself. Having compassion for others is a tremendous gift not only to them, but amazingly enough, to yourself as well. What you resonate out to the world in compassion, contentment, and courage will also boomerang back to you with multiple force. Know this and release that knowledge at the same time; give because it is the way and your purpose, not for any ulterior motive.

THIS RECIPE OF

METTA SELF-LOVE,

AND

SEVA SELFLESS-SERVICE,

IS A

superfood

OF SPIRITUAL CONTENTMENT AND EVOLUTION.

Ask yourself in any situation, *how can I be of service? How can I help?* If you are only focused on your own needs you will fester and churn inward without the freedom and release of joy in action. Simultaneous self-study coupled with service out in the world is the recipe for abundance and contentment, especially when times are difficult.

This *fierce kindness* philosophy of service and compassion is the essence of releasing "destination thinking," or only thinking about the end result, and enjoying the ride or jour-ney. Be content in all the imperfect circumstances in which you find yourself, and create the kindest mindset possible.

imperfection,
CAN BE
beautiful.

CHAPTER FOUR

CHANGE

- your -

LIFE

Change:
TAKE ACTION
TO SHIFT, MOVE, TRANSFORM

Now that you have entered the practice of choosing to see the goodness in and around you, and are training your eyes to see what is right, beautiful, kind, and hopeful, you can see the potential in any given situation, and are ready to move forward.

This chapter offers clear tools to help you guide your life in the direction you would like it to go, to be bold, and bloom.

BE
BOLD

and

BLOOM.

You now know that you have the power to choose how you think, focus your attention, and create a sense of well-being. You do not have to be a victim of your circumstances. **Do not confuse your *core self* with your current circumstances.** You are not a boss or a wife or a son or daughter. You are not poor or wealthy but simply a person who is lovable and someone who can be a positive part of the world and relationships no matter the current circumstances of your life. You are on a journey.

Many aspects of your life are in a continuing state of flux. That's not only okay, it's interesting. Curiosity will create possibility and help you to objectively enjoy your life's experiences rather than judging them. Focus on the unique, intriguing experiences you are having along your personal journey.

Your life is like a road trip, and your *core self* is posting directions and helpful road signs for you, and when you ignore them you get lost. Being lost sucks, so here we go with new daily habits that, like a map, will help you **take charge, be heard,** and **turn fear to love.** In other words, it will help you live your life with *fierce kindness.*

PAUSE AND LISTEN

The power is in the pause
to feel and observe your thoughts.

 *Ways to Pause* • • • • • • • • • • • • • • • •

BEGINNING AND ENDING PAUSE

Begin and end your day with a reset and a direction of intention. Pause after you wake and consciously stay still, feel, and listen, then count your blessings. Start with gratitude and then create a positive vision of your day that is in alignment with your goals, loves, and joys in your life. It is the same in reverse before sleep: pause, take deep breaths, and count your blessings. Then create a positive vision of your goals, loves, and life dreams.

TRANSITION PAUSE

Transitions and in-between moments are an excellent time to develop mindfulness and inner listening. A transition pause can be practiced when moving from one place to another. Use this pause to get clear on what is desired, what is needed, and to create a positive focus to move into the next moment. For example, I often pause in front of a doorway to stabilize and redirect my mind and body before I step through it. I consciously choose a positive inner statement or affirmation that is in alignment with my purpose. When I walk into the studio where I teach during the week, I may use an inner statement such as, "I am ready to be of service."

REPETITIVE PAUSE

Set a gentle chime alarm, or wear a simple bracelet or string on your wrist, to remind you to stop where you are to feel and listen. Just pause, drop whatever you are doing, notice how you are feeling, and then identify your inner dialogue. If it is negative, take a moment to refocus it to positive. Do this once an hour throughout the day. Add a celebration of your ability to begin again and the additional conscious gratitude will super-infuse this pause.

EMOTION PAUSE

Pause when you feel angry, frustrated, grouchy, bored, weepy, agitated, worried, uncomfortable, sleepy (and it is not time for sleep), hungry (and you just ate), or confused. Stop where you are, stand or sit up straight, be still, listen to your inner voice, and notice how you feel. Either journal or make a mental note of when during your day you find yourself in a state of reactivity instead of in charge of your thoughts and feelings. That is a cue that your *core self* is calling for attention and redirection. These feelings are not to be denied, they are to be acknowledged, as they are messages and fuel for growth.

CUED PAUSE

Pause when you say out loud (or internally), "I have to," "I should," "but," "always," "never," "everything," "it's always like this," "you never," or "everything is wrong." Pause when you catch yourself blaming someone else for your state of being or situation. Be especially attentive to gossip, complaining, and comparisons, as these are thoughts coupled with the power of action, and you will reap as you sow—this is a call to be a special gardener here. Notice, refocus, and move to the intentional love and empathy.

SAVORING PAUSE

Add five seconds of a pause to concentrate on and savor any moment or action that is important. Add it to every hug, kiss, eye gaze, hand hold, with every loved one, especially your children. Add it before any important response or answer, especially in a challenging conversation. Add it before a bite of food. Add it times ten before responding to a text or email (so about a minute at least). Use it to slow down time and be fully present.

Use these pauses to feel and listen and check in with your *core self* to consciously create your mindset and actions.

RESET

Take charge and

shift from *fear* to love.

Ways to Shift ● ● ● ● ● ● ● ● ● ● ● ● ● ● ● ● ●

COUNT YOUR BLESSINGS AND BE GRATEFUL

Gratitude is like an amazing grease cutter: use it to cut through the dirt and grime of your fear and anxiety. Count your blessings; start with something seemingly simple such as a bed to sleep in or fresh water to drink. These basic blessings are actually very big. They may stop you in your tracks and reset any negative thoughts right away. You are already blessed and have much to be thankful for. Build from there and keep counting blessings until you feel shifted and uplifted.

CELEBRATE

Celebration is a form of gratitude; celebrate every chance you get for every bit of the positive, no special holiday needed. When you celebrate (however small) it expands and magnetizes joy, both for you and others. Write down what you are grateful for and post it where you can see it. Thank others freely and consider keeping a gratitude journal. I am grateful that you are joining me in this practice of *fierce kindness.*

LOOK FOR GOODNESS

Train your eyes to see what is good and right in any given moment and shift perspective if needed. Practice pausing and then looking for what is working or the positive that will help you shift into possibility.

PRACTICE DETACHED CURIOSITY

Look with detached interest as if watching a movie of whatever or whoever is present. Be curious about what may have come before, or how it was created; look for what is interesting, beautiful, innocent, or important and then proceed with this new insight.

UTILIZE THE LENS OF NEW AND DELIGHT

See everything anew. Practice shifting the lens and looking with fresh eyes at everything and everyone you are seeing. See the sky, trees, husband, children, and all humans in front of you with a first-time lens and then delight in them. You can add the inner exclamation of "how delightful..." and see a new, beautiful detail that you may have missed once before. Savor and explore with renewed curiosity.

SWITCH THE MESSAGE

Say it in the positive. The words you say can change your mindset and how you feel. You can change your mind by repeating the positive form of what you want. Take the statement you are telling yourself that is negative and turn it around. Change:

"I can't do this," into "I can do this."

"I give up," into
"What tool can I use to help myself?"

"I don't understand," into "What am I missing?"

Utilize "I am" connected to a positive declaration as it creates a statement of power. Anything after "I am" will be magnetized.

"I am courageous."

"I am ready."

"I am powerful when I am kind."

Use these affirmations or positive statements with repetition: once you've said it positively, repeat it (silently or aloud). Repetition is key in changing new thought patterns in your brain. Repeat, repeat, repeat at least ten times at minimum and build to 108 or more.

DUMP THE MENTAL EMOTIONAL GARBAGE

Detox and eliminate the negative. Cry, talk (trash talking won't help), make noise, pound a pillow, journal it out to create space to feel, and then shift yourself to the positive. Sometimes it is essential to eliminate before redirecting our thinking.

FORGIVE (YOURSELF AND ALL OTHERS)

Choose to forgive and rewrite a story around a challenging occurence in your life. Look at what you learned and how you have become clearer from the experience. It is not a condoning of bad behavior but rather an expansion of vision. What does not kill you makes you stronger and you are very much alive, so now look back and be grateful for the lessons or diamonds that have been left by the intensity of the experience. Count the lessons as blessings, and genuinely wish healing and happiness for the person or people connected with this experience. Meditate on the feeling in your heart, imagine your heart is tied up with the string of connection from this person or experience and then visualize untying that string and purposely letting it go.

LIGHTEN UP

Let it go. Laugh it off. Just say "oh well" and stop caring quite as much. See the situation from a distance or as a game and play with it with a sense of curiosity. Imagine the situation in the ridiculous; I often imagine all involved in '80s hot pink spandex and that will shift it almost immediately. Do or watch something that makes you laugh.

SIT STILL

Simply sit quietly and concentrate on gratitude or beauty: a beautiful object that inspires you, a flower, flame, or even simply the in and out of your breath. Concentrate your focus in stillness and watch your thoughts go by like clouds in the sky. Observe and allow. This will reset your state of being as well as help you hear your intuition and innate wisdom to make more refined choices in your life.

INVESTIGATE FOR INTRIGUE

Look and listen for the lesson that is being delivered to you. There is always an intriguing message, a kernel of goodness being shown and being shared with you. Each interaction and happening has wisdom to bestow—for you and from you. Reciprocally you are being given, as well as always delivering, a message to others. The message is always in the love channel; sometimes it may be the need to consciously release the fear or doubt that is being shared with you in exchange for the increased power of choosing love and faith. Listen and align with the love channel. Receive and give consciously.

BE OF SERVICE AND TAKE A STAND

Ask, how can I help? Look for ways to be of service to others. Seva, or selfless service, is an amazing energy and life changer. Don't wait until your life is perfect. Go help another right now as it will attract abundance in to your life. Consider joining a local, national or global organization that takes a stand for a cause you believe in.

HELP YOURSELF
AND BOOST YOUR CONFIDENCE

Where are you consciously and unconsciously harming your body, mind, and spirit? This may be a pain point area as well as an area where you may feel out of control or toxic. Think bad habits, think being around negative people or situations, think of fear-based TV and movies, etc. Consciously remove, change, or shift something small: instead of TV, read a book that inspires you. Drink a glass of water first thing in the morning. Go to sleep a half hour earlier or put away electronics after dinner to begin to up-grade your self-care. Not sure where to eliminate or what to address? Change what feels the most like fear, anger, or depletion. Remember the visceral exercise of feeling your body in connection to thoughts (fear or love). Feelings are stronger than thoughts. Take a moment, sit quietly, feel your emotional body when you think about a certain aspect of your life that is in question. Start there to form the simple habit of supporting yourself better. You will feel proud of yourself that you are following through and taking better care. This feeling of pride coupled with the in-creased positivity will take your courage and confidence to a new high vibration. Like attracts like and this will expand upon itself.

WEAVE MAGIC INTO THE MUNDANE

Appreciation and gratitude are magical. Practice being thankful for everything that you do, touch, and have while weaving greater love awareness into it. For example, I consciously tidy the bedroom I share with my husband with thankfulness. I don't just make the bed; I bless our bed and appreciate it for the safety and comfort it gives us. I straighten, tighten, wipe, clear, and touch with eyes and hands of love and gratitude. I chop, sauté, and stir with thankfulness for the food and family that I am serving as well as the nourishment for my own body. This practice did not come effortlessly to me: I had to choose to switch complaints for a loving awareness around my actions, and consciously create an open mind-heart. When I weave this appreciation and service into the mundane, I experience great nourishment and sacred connection that feels like magic and energizes me. This is also a wonderful place to weave in a positive affirmation or declaration of intent.

VISUALIZE AND ASK FOR WHAT YOU WANT

"Worrying is a prayer for what you don't want." I am not sure who originally said this but I wholeheartedly agree. Put your energy, mind, and efforts towards what you want to create. What you feed will grow, and nourishing, visualizing, declaring, and requesting what you want will bring it to you. Catch any manipulation of your desires, and all complaining when you think about and discuss what you don't want, and weed it. Practice by being direct with yourself: I want, I envision, I imagine (say it out loud and write it down). Practice with others as well, especially those with whom you are in close relationships, and tell them exactly what you want. Don't make them guess, don't wait for them to figure it out; spell it out for them with crystal clarity. Spell it out for yourself and others to make it happen.

ASK FOR HELP

Our work is about being self-accountable, and yet there are times it is imperative we reach out to the mentors and trusted friends around us. If you feel overwhelmed and unable to utilize the tools offered here, please ask for help. Reach out to a trusted friend or teacher, a possible mentor who is doing and sharing the work you aspire to, or an emotional or mental health professional. You are not alone and we are here to help. Join a support group of like-minded individuals or start your own to create a circle of *fierce kindness* support.

CHAPTER FIVE

RIPPLE EFFECT

RIPPLE EFFECT:

THE INFLUENCE AND EFFECT
OF *FIERCE KINDNESS*
TO CHANGE THE WORLD.

Fierce Kindness:

ONE an action of powerful goodness that shifts the inner conversation from negative to positive; problem to possibility; fear to *love*

TWO a choice to be kind, especially when it's difficult

THREE a movement of nonviolence and *global conscious-ness shifting*

TURN A PROBLEM INTO A POSSIBILITY, A NEGATIVE TO A POSITIVE, FEAR TO *love*, TO CONSCIOUSLY SHIFT *your life* AND THE WORLD.

This is a call to action: change your own and the world's negatives to positives, be a catalyst for love and an integral part of the *fierce kindness* movement. Here is a place to begin to go and do. It contains a list of activities for you, your family, local community, and global posse. These are just some of the tools to shift yourself, your community, and the world from scarcity to abundance and turn *fear* to *love*.

THIS IS
a call to action
TO
STAND UP
AGAINST VIOLENCE, INJUSTICE AND DARKNESS.
CHANGE
STARTS WITH YOU.

Remember only one person is needed to be a catalyst for peace, and that person is you. My mama often told me, "Mel, be a leader, not a follower." Dear friend, be a leader, not a follower. It is okay that you are not perfect and are a work in progress. We are all works in progress. Choose to begin again and lead the way in goodness. You don't have to be perfect or finished to lead; you have to believe in something greater than yourself. **Believe without a doubt in love and goodness to give you the courage to be the change in the world.** Your efforts may or may not be met with immediately visible outcomes, but rest assured that no kind gesture is too small to have an impact. Be fierce in your belief in love, kindness, positivity, and that you are a part of the solution for the world. Your kindness may not seem to land while you are present, yet it will indeed have a ripple effect, so stay the course, have faith and rise up to be a positive force of change in the world.

There is a ripple effect for everything that we do—intentionally or unintentionally, so let's *intentionally* set forth a powerful force of kindness. Through our skilled actions of positivity, **let us begin to reverberate goodness throughout the world.** You will reach hundreds, thousands, and maybe even millions with your seemingly simple acts of kindness. By seeing the good around you, seeing the goodness inside other human beings, and acknowledging and acting upon that goodness, you will begin a domino effect of sight, acknowledgment, and shift of local and global consciousness for the better: from negative to positive, from problem to possibility, and from *fear* to *love*.

Give more than you take and in any situation, and ask yourself, "How can I serve? How can I give here?" **Leave life better than when you found it by consciously engaging in the world around you with curiosity and leadership.**

Universal Principles of Fierce Kindness:

Change your thoughts to shift your life.

Love works by faith. Doubt is the work of fear and causes suffering.

Do it and you will become it.

What you think, say, and do has power.

You co-create your experience; it does not happen to you.

Worrying focuses on what you don't want, so train your mind to visualize the highest outcome.

Love and gratitude resonate with a ripple effect.

Everything is connected.

Like attracts like.

What you focus on expands.

Happiness and love are choices.

Problems are **possibilities** to strengthen and fulfill life's purpose.

Believe in love 100% to manifest it.

Accountability of experience creates **power**.

What you look for you will find.

Give without expectation of return.

Align with kindness and you will manifest great power.

Give more than you take.

Curiosity is a possibility creator.

Ahead is a chart of actions to get you started on your journey towards a *fierce kindness* takeover. If you would like to substitute activities you prefer, feel free to do so. There is no need to choose these in order, unless that is what you are called to do.

Close your eyes and put a finger on a day, or scan the activity list to feel which speaks to you and creates the most excitement. However you do it, choose a daily action and take a moment to sit with it. Pause to visualize it and allow it to move a positive vibration through your body. **Write down your commitment to follow through with the activity.** Repeat your commitment in the form of an affirmation throughout the day or during the month. Do it until you become it.

Being of service and sharing kindness is less about *what* you give and more about *how* you give: give boldly and with true love. Don't hold back, be transparent, be fearless, lead the way. Share your love and consider keeping a journal of your *fierce kindness* explorations, including how and when they shifted your mindset and contentment.

This practice is fully one of *Metta* (self-love and kindness) and *Seva* (selfless outward service). **Giving out the love you seek will transform you.** Like a muscle, work it and it will get stronger. Do it and you will become it.

Go back to it, celebrate it, and share with those you care about. **The more you do it, the more you will get** a positive feedback loop going to create new habits that are in alignment with your highest *core self*.

Inspiring Fierce Kindness:
Daily Actions and Affirmations for One Month

DAY 1 Join an organization that is making positive change in the world. *"Together we can create a kindness revolution."*

DAY 2 Make gentle eye contact with everyone you see (friend or stranger) and see their innate goodness. *"We are all doing the best we can and are in it together."*

DAY 3 Volunteer at a local organization that is helping those in need. *"One person at a time and it starts with me."*

DAY 4 Practice listening, to understand what someone you care about needs, and then offer to help and support them. *"I am strong and I can help."*

DAY 5 Bring coloring books and crayons to leave in a hospital waiting room or the children's wing. *"I am creative and know how to surprise and delight."*

DAY 6 Donate blood. *"I am powerful and share my vitality."*

DAY 7 Pick up litter, tidy thrown paper in a public restroom, or do a chore for a friend or family member. *"I will leave all better than when I found it."*

DAY 8 Leave short notes of appreciation for family, coworkers, and community service people (like the postman or delivery person). *"I am thankful of all I have and will show gratitude to others."*

DAY 9 Look up and smile at everyone you see (smiles are contagious). *"We are all in it together."*

DAY 10 Write or call your elected official to make your voice heard about the need for community, equality and environmental support. *"My voice makes a difference."*

DAY 11 Ask for help and allow that person to be of service to you. *"I am supported."*

DAY 12 Help someone in need (packing groceries, opening and holding the door, carrying packages). *"Being of service makes me happy and I am ready to help."*

DAY 13 Carry spare change or small bills in your pocket to give away to people who need it; give it all away by the end of the day or purchase a gift card when you check out at a store and then give it as a gift to the checker who rang it for you. *"I am abundant and it makes me happy to share."*

DAY 14 Bring your pet to visit a local nursing home. *"Love and kindness create more love and kindness."*

DAY 15 Say hello, smile, and delight in every child and mother you see. *"I see the goodness in all I meet. We are all the same and desiring of love and acceptance."*

DAY 16 Give someone else the right of way, the parking spot, the seat on the train or bus, the space in line. *"I have enough and I am happy to share."*

DAY 17 Express gratitude to those who have helped you become who you are. Start with your parents, grandparents, siblings, teachers; aim for five people. *"I am thankful for all who have created who I am."*

DAY 18 Give new pajamas, new athletic shoes, or new toys to a home for foster children. *"I have more than enough."*

DAY 19 Bring special treats to the fire station and/or the police department. *"I am a leader in sweetness and love to delight."*

DAY 20 Offer your special talent (instrument, singing, magic, dance, origami) to a nursing home, children's hospital, or long-term care facility. *"I am resourceful and I can help."*

DAY 21 Pay it forward: pay for the coffee, the toll, the grocery bill, the meal of the person beside you or behind you in line. *"May my actions surprise, delight, and bless all whom I come in contact with."*

DAY 22 Donate warm clothing (socks, coats, mittens, hats), shoes, a KIND bag of new unwrapped toiletries to a homeless shelter or women's or family shelter. *"If one of us is suffering, all of us are suffering."*

DAY 23: Lead with the positive, start conversations with what is really working about the situation, the day, the moment. You can phrase this with gratitude. *"I can see the goodness in all things."*

DAY 24 Go to an animal shelter to hold an animal and walk dogs. *"Love is our universal language."*

DAY 25 Plant a tree or plant. (Work the soil with your hands and water it when finished.) *"I am part of the solution."*

DAY 26 Actively forgive three people; start with yourself. Say out loud, *"I forgive you,"* *"I release the pain of this event,"* *"I am thankful for the lessons it has taught me,"* *"I wish you to be healthy, happy, and free,"* *"All of life has brought me to this point of grace and abundance."*

DAY 27 Hold a family, friend, and work meeting to discuss an important topic you and they may be avoiding, the one that can make a difference for the better. *"I am ready to be an architect of change."*

DAY 28: Find a chance to help your neighbor: shovel snow, bring a garbage can in from the curb, rake their leaves, walk their dog, offer to run an errand (great for a new mom, the elderly or ill). *"I am strong and support for my community."*

DAY 29 Write a hand-written thank-you note and deliver or send it. Say a genuine thank you with eye contact to all the helpers throughout your day. *"I am grateful for this global village."*

DAY 30 Offer acknowledgement for effort, kindness, and goodness to the people around you; aim for five times in a day. *"I am a witness to the power of kindness."*

DAY 31 Bless all who come in your presence. Send the person a blessing whether they smile at you or they cut you off in traffic. Think and say to yourself: *"May you be happy, healthy, and free."* Bless yourself and all you meet, especially when it is difficult. I will often add, in a situation where the person has done something aggressive in traffic or a crowd, *"You must be having a difficult time."* And then, *"May you be happy, healthy, and free."* By blessing that person instead of resenting them, you will bless yourself and nourish your own abundance. *"I am love."*

FIERCE KINDNESS

is an action of powerful goodness that
shifts the inner conversation
from negative to positive; problem to
possibility; *fear* to *love*. It is choosing
to be *kind*, especially when difficult,
and a movement of nonviolence
for *global consciousness shifting.*

FIERCE KINDNESS

is a way of life for yourself, for others,
and for the world; the possibilities are
unlimited. You have great power to affect
your life and the world for the better.

This is just the beginning: your power and clarity will continue to grow and the ripple effect is infinite. Rise up to share your love and fierce kindness to be a positive force for change far and wide.

– *Thank you* –
FOR JOINING ME,
JOINING US,
IN THIS
UPRISING OF GOODNESS.

There are more resources where I virtually live: MelanieSalvatoreAugust.com

With love and ***fierce kindness,***

Mel

Library of Congress Cataloging-in-Publication Data available upon request.

ISBN 978-0-9905370-9-0

Manufactured in Hong Kong.

This book has been set in Minimo, Racon, and Festivo.

Published by Yellow Pear Press, LLC.
yellowpearpress.com

10 9 8 7 6 5 4 3 2 1

Distributed by Publishers Group West.

Acknowledgements

I am thankful for this life, for the love that is in and around me. I am thankful for all of the people who have helped me grow and share what is deep in my heart-mind. I am in wonder of the power of connection with soul purpose and I am so incredibly thankful for all of you near and far. Extra-special fierce thanks to Rafael August (my husband), Giovanni August, Casciato August, and Roman August (my boys), Phyllis and Pat Salvatore (my beloved parents), Joan and Boyer August (my beloved second parents), Lisa McGuinness (publisher and woman extraordinaire), Tracy Sunrize Johnson (for her magical design), Anne Bentley (for her insightful artwork), Dina Muth (and family), Jeff Salvatore (and family), the entire Franciosa/August clan, Ashley Cunnane, Kortney Larson, Julie Conrad, Mynx Inatsugu, Jessica Boylston-Fagonde, Kaitlin Pratt, Colleen Millen, Amber Hazor, Jill Spratt, Rachelle Abreu, Kathe Oster, Emily Cardamon, Amber Hogue, Gene Norris, Ann Modine, Elena Brower, all of my YogaWorks and lululemon family. Every one of the generous friends who support Fierce Kindness, who come to practice yoga and explore *core self* with me each day and every week. The many everyday heroes and cheerleaders around me, *all of you*, you know who you are. Everyone who believes in the power of goodness and who is courageous enough to join the movement, this way of life called *fierce kindness*.

A Few Resources

Climate Change and African Wildlife **awf.org**

Climate Change and Environmental Protection **edf.org**

Defend our Wildlife **defenders.org**

Equal Rights and Tolerance **aclu.org**

Fighting Hunger Worldwide **wfp.org**

Global Women's Equality **globalfundforwomen.org**

Green and Peaceful Earth **greenpeace.org/usa**

Humanitarian Aid and Development **ifrc.org**

Humanitarian Aid for Children **unicef.org**

Mata Amritanandamayi **amma.org**

Protect the World's Oceans **oceana.org**

Social Justice in the Classroom **teachingforchange.org**

Spreading Kindness **randomactsofkindness.org**

Thich Nhat hanh **thanhfoundation.org**

Water Conservation **wateruseitwisely.com**

Vitarka badhane pratipaksha bhavanam.

"When disturbed by negative thoughts,
opposite positive ones should be thought of.
This is pratipaksha bhavanam."

● ● ● ● ● ● ● ● ● ● ●

Ahimsa pratisthayam tat samnidhau vaira tyagah.

"In the presence of one firmly established in non-violence,
all hostilities cease."

● ● ● ● ● ● ● ● ● ● ●

Patanjali's Sutras; 2:33 and 2:35

● ● ● ● ● ● ● ● ● ● ●

Circa 400BC English translation from
The Yoga Sutras of Patanjali (Sri Swami Satchidananda)

Melanie Salvatore-August is the creator of **Fierce Kindness**,
a movement of nonviolence and global consciousness shifting.
She is also the author of *Kitchen Yoga: Simple Home Practices
to Transform Mind, Body and Life*. In addition, she is a yoga and meditation
teacher/trainer mentor for Yogaworks, CTA Yoga-Based Life Coach,
Reiki healer, lululemon Brand Ambassador, wife to her beloved
Rafael August and a mama to three little boys. She lives in the
SF Bay Area on her budding urban homestead. Find her virtually at
melaniesalvatoreaugust.com.

Also by Melanie Salvatore-August:

An inspiring twist on integrating yoga and life, *Kitchen Yoga* cooks up poses
and practices to do wherever you are, from a modified down dog while
waiting for your morning coffee to steep, to detox practices in the bathroom,
locust pose in the living room, and many more. Finish your day with relaxation exercises
in bed and slip into a calm, peaceful sleep. Easy-to-follow yoga "recipes"
coupled with helpful illustrations will transform your simmering, stress-filled life
into a feast for the mind and body.